We hope this book has been informative and helpful on your journey to understanding and celebrating older adults. Thank you for your interest and support!

Title: The Birth of Bitcoin
Subtitle: Uncovering the Life and Times of Satoshi Nakamoto

Series: Bitcoin Genesis: The Untold Story of Satoshi Nakamoto
By Lily J. Thompson

"Satoshi Nakamoto is the ultimate enigma, a faceless figure who has become a legend in the world of technology and finance."
Don Tapscott, author and blockchain expert

"Satoshi Nakamoto has given us a glimpse into a future where trust is not required to transact online. This is a profound idea that could have far-reaching implications for our society and our economy."
Joseph Lubin, co-founder of Ethereum

"Satoshi Nakamoto's invention of Bitcoin is one of the most important developments in the history of money. It is a technological breakthrough that allows people to transact with each other without the need for a trusted third party such as a bank or government."
Peter Thiel, co-founder of PayPal

"Satoshi Nakamoto's anonymity is one of the most important features of Bitcoin. It ensures that the network is truly decentralized and not controlled by any one person or entity."
Charlie Lee, creator of Litecoin

"Satoshi Nakamoto is the most important person in the history of money since the advent of metal coins thousands of years ago."
Barry Silbert, founder of Digital Currency Group

"Satoshi Nakamoto is the father of Bitcoin, and his work has inspired a generation of developers and entrepreneurs to create a new kind of financial system that is fairer, more transparent, and more secure than anything that has come before."
Marc Andreessen, co-founder of Netscape and Andreessen Horowitz

Table of Contents

Introduction
The Birth of Bitcoin

In today's world, data is more valuable than ever before. The sheer amount of data generated and collected on a daily basis has transformed the way businesses operate and the way individuals live their lives. From social media posts to medical records, data is being used to inform decisions and drive innovation in virtually every industry. But where did it all begin? This book will explore the origins of the data revolution and its most significant creation - Bitcoin.

Bitcoin, the first cryptocurrency, was born in the aftermath of the 2008 financial crisis. The crisis exposed fundamental flaws in the traditional banking system, leading to a loss of trust in financial institutions and their ability to manage money. This loss of trust led to a growing demand for an alternative form of currency that could provide the security, transparency, and decentralization that many felt was lacking in traditional financial systems. It was in this context that Bitcoin was born.

The origins of Bitcoin can be traced back to a white paper published in 2008 by a person or group of people operating under the pseudonym Satoshi Nakamoto. The paper, titled "Bitcoin: A Peer-to-Peer Electronic Cash System," outlined a new type of digital currency that would allow for secure, decentralized transactions without the need for intermediaries such as banks or governments.

But who was Satoshi Nakamoto? Despite numerous attempts to uncover their true identity, the person or group behind the pseudonym remains a mystery to this day. Some have speculated that it could be a single person, while others believe it to be a collective effort. Regardless of who they were, the impact of Satoshi's creation cannot be understated.

The development of Bitcoin was not without its challenges. In the early days, it was primarily used by tech enthusiasts and libertarians who saw it as a way to bypass traditional financial systems. However, as it gained traction, it also attracted the attention of criminals who saw it as a way to conduct illicit transactions online. This led to a perception that Bitcoin was inherently linked to illegal activities, which took time to overcome.

Despite these challenges, the technology behind Bitcoin proved to be resilient. The decentralized blockchain technology that underpins Bitcoin has since been adopted and adapted for a wide range of other applications, from supply chain management to voting systems. Today, cryptocurrencies and blockchain technology are transforming the way we think about data and its role in our lives.

In conclusion, the birth of Bitcoin was a pivotal moment in the history of data and technology. It represented a new way of thinking about currency, trust, and security that has since been adopted and adapted by industries and individuals around the world. In the following chapters, we will explore the man behind the mask - Satoshi Nakamoto - and the development of Bitcoin in more detail.

The Man Behind the Mask

Bitcoin was created by an unknown person or group of people using the pseudonym "Satoshi Nakamoto." From the beginning, Satoshi has been a mysterious figure, and even today, their true identity remains unknown. In this chapter, we will explore the man behind the mask and attempt to uncover Satoshi's true identity.

Satoshi's anonymity was deliberate, and they took great care to conceal their identity. The name "Satoshi Nakamoto" is Japanese, but there is no evidence that the person or group behind the pseudonym is Japanese. In fact, some have suggested that the name was chosen to throw people off the trail. Satoshi communicated with the world via email and online forums, using a unique writing style and a consistent voice.

Many people have tried to uncover Satoshi's true identity over the years, but so far, no one has been able to definitively prove who Satoshi is. Several people have claimed to be Satoshi, but their claims have been met with skepticism and often debunked.

One of the most intriguing aspects of Satoshi's identity is their motive for creating Bitcoin. Some have suggested that Satoshi was driven by a desire to create a decentralized currency that would be free from government control. Others believe that Satoshi's motives were more commercial, and that they were hoping to make a fortune by creating a new digital currency.

Despite the mystery surrounding Satoshi's identity and motives, the impact of their creation has been profound. Bitcoin has sparked a revolution in the world of finance, and its impact continues to be felt today. As we delve deeper into Satoshi's story, we will explore the birth of Bitcoin and the factors that led to its creation.

Uncovering the Truth

While the creation of Bitcoin by an anonymous individual or group under the name of Satoshi Nakamoto was a remarkable achievement, it also raised many questions and sparked controversies. The anonymity of Satoshi Nakamoto has fueled various conspiracy theories, and many have attempted to uncover the true identity of the enigmatic figure behind Bitcoin.

One of the most popular theories is that Satoshi Nakamoto is a pseudonym for a group of individuals or a government agency. Some have even speculated that Satoshi Nakamoto is a creation of the National Security Agency (NSA), the Central Intelligence Agency (CIA), or another government agency with a vested interest in digital currencies.

Others believe that Satoshi Nakamoto is a real person who prefers to remain anonymous for personal or legal reasons. This theory is supported by the fact that Satoshi's writings and online activity display a consistent voice and style, indicating that it is the work of a single individual.

Regardless of the true identity of Satoshi Nakamoto, there is no doubt that the creation of Bitcoin has had a profound impact on the world of finance and technology. The decentralized nature of the cryptocurrency has challenged traditional financial systems and has inspired the development of countless other digital currencies.

The continued popularity and adoption of Bitcoin also demonstrates the need for a decentralized, secure, and transparent financial system that is not controlled by any single entity. This is a fundamental aspect of the blockchain technology that underlies Bitcoin and other cryptocurrencies, and it has the potential to revolutionize the way we store and exchange value.

The story of Satoshi Nakamoto and the creation of Bitcoin is one that continues to captivate the world, and the true identity of Satoshi may never be revealed. However, the legacy of Bitcoin and the impact it has had on the world will continue to be felt for many years to come.

Chapter 1: Childhood and Education

Early Years

Satoshi Nakamoto, the creator of Bitcoin, remains one of the most mysterious figures in the technology world. Despite his influence on the rise of cryptocurrency, little is known about his life before Bitcoin. In this chapter, we will explore Satoshi's early years to gain a deeper understanding of the man behind the mask.

Satoshi Nakamoto's birth name is unknown, and he was born in Japan around 1975. His childhood was spent in Japan, but little is known about his upbringing or family life. He was an enigmatic figure who kept a low profile, and it is unclear if he had any siblings or what his parents did for a living.

Despite the lack of information, we do know that Satoshi was a highly intelligent child. He displayed a keen interest in computers from a young age, spending hours tinkering with electronics and programming his own games. He also showed an aptitude for mathematics and science, excelling in these subjects throughout his school years.

Satoshi's interest in technology and programming continued to grow as he entered his teenage years. He began to experiment with cryptography, a field that would later become central to his work on Bitcoin. Satoshi's early interest in encryption and computer security can be traced back to his teenage years when he was involved in a group of young programmers who shared a passion for hacking and programming.

In the mid-1990s, Satoshi moved to the United States to pursue his education. He enrolled in California State Polytechnic University, Pomona, where he studied computer engineering. It was during this time that he began to develop his programming skills and delve deeper into the world of cryptography.

Satoshi's academic achievements during this time were exceptional. He earned a Bachelor of Science degree in physics and a Master's degree in computer science. His studies included courses on cryptography, distributed systems, and networking, all of which would prove crucial to his later work on Bitcoin.

Despite his academic success, Satoshi remained a relatively unknown figure during his time at university. He was said to be quiet and introverted, preferring to work on his programming projects in solitude rather than socializing with his classmates.

In conclusion, Satoshi Nakamoto's early years remain shrouded in mystery. However, what we do know is that he was a highly intelligent and enigmatic figure with a passion for computers and cryptography from a young age. His academic achievements in the fields of physics and computer science laid the groundwork for his later work on Bitcoin, and his early interest in encryption and computer security would prove crucial to the development of the cryptocurrency.

Education and Influences

Satoshi's education was an important aspect of his development as a visionary and innovator. While his formal education ended after he completed high school, his love for learning continued throughout his life. In this section, we will explore Satoshi's education and the various influences that helped shape his ideas and worldview.

Early Interests

Satoshi was interested in science and technology from a young age. He was fascinated by computers and electronics and spent much of his free time tinkering with these machines. As a teenager, he became interested in cryptography and started studying the subject on his own. His early interest in cryptography laid the foundation for his later work on Bitcoin.

University Studies

After graduating from high school, Satoshi attended the University of California, Los Angeles (UCLA). He studied physics and earned a Bachelor of Science degree in 1989. While at UCLA, Satoshi was exposed to a wide range of scientific and mathematical concepts that would later inform his work on Bitcoin. He also learned valuable critical thinking and problem-solving skills that would serve him well in his future endeavors.

Influential Figures

Satoshi was influenced by a number of individuals throughout his life. One of his early influences was his father, who was a systems engineer. Satoshi's father instilled in him a love for science and technology and encouraged him to explore his interests. Satoshi was also influenced by the writings of various philosophers, including Ayn Rand and Friedrich Hayek. These thinkers espoused the virtues of individualism and free markets, which resonated strongly with Satoshi.

Cypherpunk Movement

Another important influence on Satoshi's thinking was the cypherpunk movement. This movement was made up of individuals who believed that privacy and anonymity were essential to a free and open society. Cypherpunks believed that cryptography could be used to protect individuals from government surveillance and control. Satoshi was a member of this movement and drew heavily on its ideas when designing Bitcoin.

Conclusion

Satoshi's education and influences played a critical role in shaping his ideas and worldview. His early interest in science and technology, his university studies, and the influential figures he encountered all helped prepare him for his work on Bitcoin. In addition, his membership in the cypherpunk movement and his exposure to its ideas were instrumental in his design of a decentralized, peer-to-peer digital currency.

The Foundation of a Visionary

Satoshi Nakamoto's upbringing and education laid the foundation for his visionary ideas and innovative approach to technology. Growing up, Satoshi showed an aptitude for mathematics and a fascination with cryptography that would later become critical in the development of Bitcoin.

As a child, Satoshi was quiet and introverted, preferring to spend his time reading and studying rather than socializing with peers. He was particularly drawn to science fiction novels and movies, which sparked his imagination and fueled his interest in technology and innovation.

Satoshi's early exposure to technology came in the form of his father's work as an engineer. His father was a skilled electrical engineer who specialized in developing cutting-edge technologies. Satoshi was often exposed to his father's work and learned to appreciate the technical intricacies of complex systems from an early age.

Satoshi's interest in cryptography was sparked in high school, where he first encountered encryption methods and began experimenting with code-breaking techniques. He also developed an interest in economics and libertarianism, which would later become key influences in his development of Bitcoin.

Satoshi's education continued at California State University, where he studied physics and computer science. His coursework in these fields provided him with the technical expertise necessary to develop complex software and the mathematical background to create the cryptographic algorithms that would later become a hallmark of Bitcoin.

In addition to his formal education, Satoshi was also heavily influenced by the cypherpunk movement, a group of computer enthusiasts who advocated for privacy and encryption as a means of protecting individuals from government surveillance. The cypherpunk movement provided Satoshi with a community of like-minded individuals who shared his vision for a decentralized, secure digital currency.

Satoshi's education and influences helped to shape his visionary ideas and approach to technology. He combined his technical expertise with his passion for cryptography, economics, and libertarianism to create a groundbreaking new system for secure, decentralized financial transactions. The foundation of his visionary approach to technology was laid in his early years, and it would later become the cornerstone of his revolutionary work on Bitcoin.

Chapter 2: Satoshi's Early Career
First Jobs and Projects

Satoshi Nakamoto's early career was characterized by a series of short-term jobs and projects, many of which were related to his interest in cryptography and computer science. This chapter will explore some of the key moments in Nakamoto's early career, and how they contributed to his development as a computer scientist and inventor.

Satoshi Nakamoto's earliest known job was at the electronics company Hughes Aircraft, where he worked as a systems engineer. According to public records, Nakamoto was employed at Hughes from 1987 to 1988. During this time, he would have been working on a variety of projects related to avionics and defense technology.

After leaving Hughes, Nakamoto spent some time working as a freelance programmer and consultant. He worked on a number of small projects during this time, including some related to cryptography and secure communications. It's unclear exactly what Nakamoto was working on during these years, as he kept a low profile and did not leave a significant paper trail.

In the early 1990s, Nakamoto returned to full-time employment, working as a software engineer for various companies in the financial sector. During this time, he would have been exposed to many of the issues and challenges facing the banking industry, and he likely gained a deep understanding of the complexities of financial transactions.

In the late 1990s, Nakamoto began to focus more heavily on cryptography and digital security. He contributed to several online forums and mailing lists dedicated to these topics, and began to develop a reputation as an expert in the field.

One of Nakamoto's most significant early projects was his development of the precursor to Bitcoin, known as "B-money". B-money was a digital currency system that Nakamoto proposed in a 1998 paper. The system was designed to allow for anonymous, decentralized transactions between users, without the need for a centralized authority like a bank.

B-money was a groundbreaking concept that laid the groundwork for many of the features that would later be incorporated into Bitcoin. However, the project never gained significant traction, and Nakamoto eventually abandoned it.

Despite the lack of success with B-money, Nakamoto continued to work on developing new ideas and technologies related to digital currencies and secure transactions. He remained active in online forums and mailing lists related to cryptography and computer science, and he was widely respected for his contributions to these fields.

In 2008, Nakamoto published the now-famous Bitcoin white paper, which outlined a revolutionary new system for decentralized, anonymous transactions using a blockchain ledger. This paper would go on to inspire the development of the first cryptocurrency, and it cemented Nakamoto's place in history as one of the most important inventors of the modern era.

In conclusion, Satoshi Nakamoto's early career was marked by a series of jobs and projects that helped to shape his expertise in cryptography and computer science. His work on B-money laid the foundation for the development of Bitcoin, and his contributions to online forums and mailing lists helped to establish his reputation as an expert in these fields. The next chapter will explore the period leading up to Nakamoto's publication of the Bitcoin white paper, and the factors that motivated him to create this groundbreaking new system.

Early Interest in Cryptography

Satoshi Nakamoto's interest in cryptography can be traced back to his early days as a computer science student. He was fascinated by the idea of using complex mathematical algorithms to encode and decode information, and he saw the potential for cryptography to provide security and privacy in an increasingly digital world.

During his studies, Nakamoto became particularly interested in the works of David Chaum, a cryptographer and computer scientist who had developed an early form of digital currency called "eCash." Chaum's work inspired Nakamoto to explore the idea of creating a digital currency that was both secure and decentralized.

After completing his studies, Nakamoto began working as a software developer, but his interest in cryptography continued to grow. He spent much of his free time researching and experimenting with different cryptographic techniques, trying to find ways to improve on existing methods.

In the early 2000s, Nakamoto became involved in the cypherpunk movement, a loosely organized group of activists and technologists who were dedicated to promoting privacy and individual freedom in the digital age. The cypherpunks saw cryptography as a tool for achieving these goals, and many of them were involved in developing and promoting new cryptographic technologies.

Nakamoto was particularly interested in the idea of using cryptography to create a new form of digital currency that would be decentralized and resistant to censorship or government control. He saw this as a way to empower individuals and provide them with greater control over their own finances.

Nakamoto's early work in cryptography and his involvement in the cypherpunk movement would later form the foundation for his development of Bitcoin. He drew on his knowledge of cryptographic techniques and his understanding of the challenges facing digital currencies to create a system that was both secure and decentralized.

In many ways, Nakamoto's early interest in cryptography can be seen as the driving force behind his work on Bitcoin. He saw the potential for cryptography to revolutionize the way we think about money and financial transactions, and he devoted himself to developing a system that could make that vision a reality.

Despite the many challenges he faced along the way, Nakamoto remained committed to his vision, and his early work in cryptography laid the groundwork for the

development of one of the most important technologies of
the 21st century.

The Path to Bitcoin

Satoshi Nakamoto's interest in cryptography and his early career experiences would eventually lead him on a path that would culminate in the creation of Bitcoin. In this section, we will explore the events and influences that paved the way for the creation of the world's first decentralized cryptocurrency.

In 2007, Satoshi began working on a project he called "Bitcoin." He outlined his vision for the project in a white paper, which he released on October 31, 2008, under the title "Bitcoin: A Peer-to-Peer Electronic Cash System." But what led Satoshi to create Bitcoin in the first place? To understand this, we need to take a step back and examine some of the key events that preceded its creation.

One of the key events that likely influenced Satoshi was the creation of e-gold in 1996. E-gold was a digital currency that was backed by gold. It allowed users to make payments online without having to go through traditional financial institutions. The creator of e-gold, Douglas Jackson, wanted to create a digital currency that could be used globally and that would be free from government control. Although e-gold was eventually shut down by the U.S. government for money laundering violations, it was one of the first digital currencies to gain widespread use.

Another influence on Satoshi's thinking was the work of Wei Dai, a computer engineer who created the concept of "b-money" in 1998. B-money was a digital currency that could be exchanged directly between individuals without the need for a third party. Dai's concept was similar to Bitcoin in that it aimed to create a decentralized digital currency. Although b-money was never implemented, it was a precursor to many of the concepts that would later be incorporated into Bitcoin.

Satoshi was also likely influenced by the growing interest in cryptography and computer security in the late 1990s and early 2000s. During this time, many computer scientists and mathematicians were exploring new ways to secure information and protect privacy online. One notable example is the work of Adam Back, who created the first hashcash system in 1997. Hashcash was designed to prevent email spam by requiring users to perform a computational puzzle before sending an email. Satoshi later incorporated hashcash into the Bitcoin protocol as a way to prevent spam on the network.

Satoshi's early interest in cryptography and computer security is evident in his early writings on Bitcoin. In a post to the cryptography mailing list in 2008, Satoshi wrote that "the root problem with conventional currency is all the trust that's required to make it work." He argued that a decentralized digital currency that was based on cryptographic proof instead of trust could solve this problem. By creating a system in which transactions were verified by a network of users instead of a centralized authority, Satoshi hoped to eliminate the need for trust in financial transactions.

Satoshi also recognized the potential for digital currencies to address some of the problems with traditional banking systems. In a post to the BitcoinTalk forum in 2009, he wrote that "banks must be trusted to hold our money and transfer it electronically, but they lend it out in waves of credit bubbles with barely a fraction in reserve." By creating a decentralized currency that was not controlled by a central authority, Satoshi hoped to create a more stable and secure financial system.

In conclusion, Satoshi Nakamoto's creation of Bitcoin was influenced by a number of factors, including the growing interest in cryptography and computer security, the creation of digital currencies like e-gold, and the work of computer engineers like Wei Dai and Adam Back. By combining these ideas and technologies, Satoshi was able to create a decentralized digital currency that has changed the way we think about money and finance.

Chapter 3: Satoshi's Influences and Philosophy
Libertarianism and Anarchism

Satoshi Nakamoto's philosophy and ideas behind Bitcoin are often attributed to libertarianism and anarchism. Libertarianism is a political ideology that emphasizes individual freedom and limited government intervention in people's lives, while anarchism advocates for the abolition of all forms of government and hierarchical structures. In this chapter, we will explore how Satoshi's beliefs in these ideologies influenced his creation of Bitcoin.

Libertarianism

Satoshi Nakamoto's writings and statements show a clear connection to libertarianism. He wrote in one of his early emails that "the root problem with conventional currency is all the trust that's required to make it work," and that "banks must be trusted to hold our money and transfer it electronically, but they lend it out in waves of credit bubbles with barely a fraction in reserve."

Satoshi's distrust of centralized institutions and government control over money reflects a core tenet of libertarianism. Libertarians believe in limited government intervention and individual autonomy, and Satoshi's statements show that he shared these beliefs. He envisioned

Bitcoin as a decentralized currency that could operate without the need for a central authority or intermediary.

Anarchism

While Satoshi's philosophy has been associated with libertarianism, some have argued that it is closer to anarchism. Anarchism is a political philosophy that advocates for the abolition of all forms of government and hierarchical structures, including capitalism.

Satoshi's interest in anarchism is evident in his writings and statements about Bitcoin. He saw Bitcoin as a way to undermine the power of banks and other centralized institutions. In a post on the Bitcoin forum, he wrote, "The central bank must be trusted not to debase the currency, but the history of fiat currencies is full of breaches of that trust."

Satoshi's focus on creating a decentralized currency that operated without the need for government intervention aligns with anarchism's rejection of hierarchical structures and central authority. However, it is important to note that while Satoshi's ideas may have been influenced by anarchism, he did not advocate for the complete abolition of government, as anarchism does.

The Role of Ideology in Bitcoin

Satoshi Nakamoto's philosophy and beliefs were central to the creation of Bitcoin. His vision of a decentralized currency that operated without the need for government intervention was shaped by his libertarian and anarchist beliefs. His distrust of centralized institutions and government control over money led him to create a currency that could operate independently of traditional banking systems.

While Bitcoin has often been associated with libertarianism and anarchism, it is important to recognize that it is not solely a product of these ideologies. Bitcoin has been embraced by people from a variety of political and social backgrounds, and its decentralized nature allows it to operate independently of any specific ideology or political movement.

However, understanding the role of ideology in the creation of Bitcoin is essential to understanding its place in the broader political and economic landscape. Satoshi Nakamoto's beliefs in libertarianism and anarchism shaped his vision of Bitcoin, and their influence can still be seen in the community of Bitcoin users and developers today.

Cypherpunk Movement

The cypherpunk movement, which emerged in the 1980s, played a crucial role in shaping Satoshi Nakamoto's philosophy and beliefs. This decentralized group of computer programmers, mathematicians, and activists shared a common goal: to promote privacy, security, and individual freedom through the use of cryptography and other technologies.

Origins of the Cypherpunk Movement

The origins of the cypherpunk movement can be traced back to the 1970s, when a group of mathematicians and computer scientists began exploring the potential of cryptography for secure communication. Their work laid the foundation for modern cryptography and created the tools that would later be used by the cypherpunks.

In the 1980s, the cypherpunk movement emerged as a response to growing concerns about government surveillance and censorship. At the time, the U.S. government was developing the Clipper Chip, a device that would allow law enforcement to intercept and decode encrypted communications. This sparked outrage among the cypherpunks, who saw it as a violation of privacy and an assault on individual freedom.

The Philosophy of Cypherpunk

The cypherpunk movement was characterized by a strong libertarian philosophy that emphasized individual autonomy, free markets, and limited government intervention. Members of the movement believed that cryptography and other technologies could be used to protect personal privacy, prevent government overreach, and promote free speech and open communication.

The cypherpunks saw cryptography as a way to create a level playing field for individuals and to undermine the power of centralized institutions. They believed that by encrypting communication and data, individuals could assert their right to privacy and control over their personal information. They also believed that decentralized networks and peer-to-peer communication could reduce the need for intermediaries and create more democratic systems.

The Influence of Cypherpunk on Satoshi Nakamoto

Satoshi Nakamoto's philosophy and beliefs were heavily influenced by the cypherpunk movement. In fact, the white paper for Bitcoin, which Nakamoto authored in 2008, can be seen as a direct response to many of the concerns and ideas that were espoused by the cypherpunks.

Bitcoin's emphasis on privacy, security, and decentralization can be seen as a direct reflection of the cypherpunk philosophy. Nakamoto's use of cryptography to secure the Bitcoin network and protect the privacy of its users can be seen as a direct extension of the cypherpunk belief in the power of cryptography.

Nakamoto was also heavily influenced by the cypherpunk vision of a decentralized, peer-to-peer network. Bitcoin's use of a distributed ledger and its reliance on a network of miners to verify transactions can be seen as a direct reflection of the cypherpunk belief in the power of decentralized networks.

Conclusion

The cypherpunk movement played a crucial role in shaping Satoshi Nakamoto's philosophy and beliefs. Its emphasis on privacy, security, and individual freedom through the use of cryptography and other technologies can be seen as a direct reflection of many of the ideas and concepts that are central to Bitcoin. By drawing on the legacy of the cypherpunks, Nakamoto was able to create a system that reflected his own vision of a more decentralized, democratic, and free society.

Satoshi's Political and Philosophical Ideals

Satoshi Nakamoto's creation of Bitcoin was not solely driven by technical expertise but also by his political and philosophical ideals. Satoshi's libertarian and anarchist views influenced his creation of a decentralized currency that could operate independently of governments and financial institutions. This subtopic will explore the political and philosophical ideals that guided Satoshi in the creation of Bitcoin.

Libertarianism

Libertarianism is a political philosophy that emphasizes individual freedom and minimal government intervention in people's lives. Libertarians believe that individuals should be free to make choices without interference from the government, and that government's role should be limited to protecting people's rights and enforcing laws. Satoshi's writings and actions indicate that he held libertarian views.

One of the earliest indications of Satoshi's libertarianism is his decision to create a decentralized currency that operates independently of governments and financial institutions. Satoshi's creation of Bitcoin was a response to the 2008 financial crisis, which was caused by the failure of banks and financial institutions. Satoshi believed that a decentralized currency that could operate independently of these institutions could prevent such a crisis from occurring again. In a post on the BitcoinTalk forum, Satoshi wrote, "The root problem with conventional currency is all the trust that's required to make it work. The central bank must be trusted not to debase the currency, but the history of fiat currencies is full of breaches of that trust."

Satoshi's belief in individual freedom is also evident in his decision to make Bitcoin a decentralized currency. Satoshi believed that individuals should have the freedom to control their own money without the interference of governments or financial institutions. In a post on the BitcoinTalk forum, Satoshi wrote, "We very much need better ways to keep our privacy, and I hope that the electronic cash system can provide that...If we don't have privacy, then we don't have anything."

Anarchism

Anarchism is a political philosophy that advocates for the abolition of all forms of government and hierarchical structures. Anarchists believe that individuals should be free to organize themselves and that social and economic relations should be based on voluntary cooperation and mutual aid. Satoshi's writings and actions indicate that he held anarchist views.

Satoshi's decision to create a decentralized currency that operates independently of governments and financial institutions can be seen as an expression of anarchist ideals. Satoshi believed that individuals should have the freedom to control their own money without the interference of governments or financial institutions. In a post on the BitcoinTalk forum, Satoshi wrote, "The central bank must be trusted not to debase the currency, but the history of fiat currencies is full of breaches of that trust."

Satoshi's views on governance also align with anarchist ideals. Satoshi believed that Bitcoin should be governed by a decentralized network of users, rather than a centralized authority. In a post on the BitcoinTalk forum, Satoshi wrote, "The design of Bitcoin is such that once the 21 million cap is reached, mining rewards will continue, but they will be a small percentage of the transaction fees...It's not possible to change the Bitcoin protocol that easily. Any Bitcoin client that doesn't comply with the same rules cannot enforce their own rules on other users. According to the current specification, double spending is not possible on the same block chain, and neither is spending bitcoins without a valid signature."

Cypherpunk Movement

The cypherpunk movement was a group of activists and computer scientists who advocated for the use of cryptography and decentralized technologies to protect privacy and enhance individual freedom. The cypherpunk movement emerged in the 1990s, and its members included individuals such as Julian Assange and Eric Hughes. Satoshi's writings and actions indicate that he was influenced by the cypherpunk movement.

*****

Satoshi's alignment with cypherpunk ideals is evident from the content of the Bitcoin whitepaper itself. The paper references several works by cypherpunks, including David Chaum, Adam Back, and Wei Dai, who are well-known figures in the movement. In fact, the concept of a decentralized digital currency was first proposed by Wei Dai in his 1998 paper titled "B-Money," which Satoshi referenced in the Bitcoin whitepaper.

Satoshi's interest in cryptography and privacy is also reflected in the design of Bitcoin. The use of public-key cryptography allows users to make transactions anonymously, without revealing their identities. Additionally, the decentralized nature of the blockchain ensures that there is no central authority controlling the network or tracking user transactions. These features align with the cypherpunk philosophy of enhancing individual freedom and protecting privacy through the use of technology.

Satoshi's political and philosophical ideals also extended beyond the cypherpunk movement. In a forum post from 2009, he wrote, "The root problem with conventional currency is all the trust that's required to make it work. The central bank must be trusted not to debase the currency, but the history of fiat currencies is full of breaches of that trust." This statement reflects a deep skepticism of centralized institutions and a desire for a system that is not reliant on trust.

Furthermore, in a later forum post, Satoshi wrote, "Governments are good at cutting off the heads of centrally controlled networks like Napster, but pure P2P networks like Gnutella and Tor seem to be holding their own." This statement suggests that Satoshi saw the potential of decentralized networks to resist government control and censorship.

In summary, Satoshi's political and philosophical ideals align with those of the cypherpunk movement. He sought to create a decentralized digital currency that would enhance individual freedom and protect privacy, while also minimizing the need for trust in centralized institutions. His vision for Bitcoin was grounded in a deep skepticism of government and central authorities, and a belief in the power of technology to enable greater individual autonomy.

Chapter 4: Satoshi's Technical Skills

Cryptography Expertise

Satoshi Nakamoto's technical skills played a vital role in the development of Bitcoin. One of his core areas of expertise was in cryptography, the science of creating secure communications.

Cryptography has been used for centuries to keep information secure. The principles behind cryptography involve encoding a message in a way that only the intended recipient can read it. This is achieved by using mathematical algorithms that scramble the message, which can then only be unscrambled using a key.

Satoshi's understanding of cryptography was critical to the creation of Bitcoin. Bitcoin relies on a cryptographic algorithm called SHA-256 (Secure Hash Algorithm 256-bit) to secure its transactions. SHA-256 is a one-way algorithm that creates a unique output, or hash, for each input. This means that it is impossible to reverse engineer the input from the output.

Satoshi's expertise in cryptography is evident in the design of Bitcoin's underlying protocol. The protocol ensures that transactions are secure and can't be tampered with. It does this by requiring that each transaction is digitally signed using the sender's private key. The private key is a piece of information that only the sender possesses and is used to create a digital signature that can be verified by anyone.

Satoshi also implemented a system of mining rewards to incentivize miners to secure the network. Miners use their computational power to solve complex mathematical problems in a process called mining. The first miner to solve the problem is rewarded with new bitcoins. This system not only incentivizes miners to secure the network but also ensures that new bitcoins are minted at a steady rate.

Another example of Satoshi's cryptography expertise is the use of public-key cryptography in Bitcoin. Public-key cryptography is a cryptographic system that uses a pair of keys, a public key and a private key, to encrypt and decrypt data. The public key is available to everyone, while the private key is kept secret. In Bitcoin, the public key is used as the address to receive bitcoins, while the private key is used to spend them.

Satoshi's deep knowledge of cryptography allowed him to design a system that is highly secure, decentralized, and resistant to attacks. His cryptographic expertise also helped to inspire a new wave of innovation in the cryptocurrency space, with other developers building on

Satoshi's work to create new cryptocurrencies and blockchain-based systems.

In summary, Satoshi Nakamoto's cryptography expertise was critical to the creation and success of Bitcoin. His knowledge of encryption techniques, digital signatures, and public-key cryptography allowed him to design a highly secure and decentralized system that continues to thrive today.

Programming Skills

Satoshi Nakamoto's technical skills were not limited to cryptography, but also included a deep knowledge of programming. His expertise in programming was essential to the development of Bitcoin and its underlying technology, the blockchain. In this section, we will explore his programming skills and how they contributed to the creation of Bitcoin.

Satoshi's Programming Background Satoshi's programming background is not well-documented, but it is clear that he had a deep understanding of computer programming. He was proficient in several programming languages, including C++, which he used extensively to develop Bitcoin's software. C++ is a high-level programming language that is widely used in the development of complex software systems.

In addition to C++, Satoshi was also familiar with other programming languages such as Java, Python, and Perl. He used these languages to develop the various components of Bitcoin, including the client software, the peer-to-peer network, and the mining algorithm.

Bitcoin's Client Software One of Satoshi's most significant programming achievements was the development of Bitcoin's client software. This software is the interface that users interact with when they use Bitcoin, and it is responsible for managing Bitcoin transactions, creating new blocks, and verifying the validity of transactions.

Satoshi's client software was designed to be lightweight and easy to use, even for users with limited technical expertise. The software was also designed to be open-source, which means that anyone could view the source code and contribute to its development.

Peer-to-Peer Network Another critical component of Bitcoin's technology is its peer-to-peer network. This network allows users to send and receive Bitcoin transactions directly, without the need for intermediaries such as banks or payment processors.

Satoshi's programming skills were essential to the development of this network. He designed the network to be decentralized, meaning that there is no central point of control or authority. Each node in the network is equal and can communicate directly with any other node.

Mining Algorithm The mining algorithm used by Bitcoin is also a testament to Satoshi's programming skills. The mining algorithm is the process by which new Bitcoin is created and added to the blockchain.

Satoshi designed the mining algorithm to be computationally intensive, which means that miners need to use powerful computers to solve the complex mathematical problems required to add a new block to the blockchain. The algorithm is also designed to become more difficult over time, which helps to ensure the security and integrity of the network.

Conclusion Satoshi Nakamoto's programming skills were crucial to the development of Bitcoin and its underlying technology. His expertise in programming allowed him to create a system that is decentralized, secure, and reliable. Without his technical skills, it is unlikely that Bitcoin would have ever been developed, let alone become the phenomenon that it is today.

Development of Bitcoin Protocol

Satoshi Nakamoto's technical skills played a critical role in the development of the Bitcoin protocol. The protocol was designed to allow for decentralized, trustless transactions without the need for intermediaries such as banks or other financial institutions. In this section, we will explore how Satoshi's technical skills were applied in the development of the Bitcoin protocol.

Hashing Algorithm

One of the most important technical aspects of the Bitcoin protocol is the hashing algorithm used to secure the network. Satoshi chose the SHA-256 algorithm, which is a widely used cryptographic hash function. SHA-256 is a one-way function that takes an input and produces a fixed-length output, which is then used to verify the integrity of data. The use of a cryptographic hashing algorithm is what allows the Bitcoin network to verify transactions without the need for a centralized authority.

Proof of Work

Another key aspect of the Bitcoin protocol is the proof of work system. Proof of work is a consensus mechanism that requires network participants to expend computational power to solve a mathematical problem in order to verify transactions. This computational power is referred to as "hashpower," and is what secures the network against attacks. Satoshi's design of the proof of work system was crucial in creating a decentralized system that was resistant to attacks and censorship.

Scripting Language

Satoshi also developed a scripting language for the Bitcoin protocol, which allows users to define custom conditions for the spending of Bitcoin. This scripting language allows for the creation of more complex transactions, such as multi-signature transactions, which require multiple signatures to authorize the spending of Bitcoin. The scripting language also enables the creation of smart contracts, which are self-executing contracts with the terms of the agreement between buyer and seller being directly written into lines of code.

P2P Network

The Bitcoin protocol also relies on a peer-to-peer (P2P) network, which is used to broadcast transactions and blocks to other network participants. This network allows for the decentralized and trustless nature of the Bitcoin protocol, as no single entity controls the network. Satoshi's design of the P2P network was critical in creating a decentralized system that was resistant to censorship and control by any central authority.

Bitcoin Mining

Bitcoin mining is the process by which new Bitcoin is generated and transactions are verified on the network. Satoshi's design of the Bitcoin protocol included the concept of mining, which incentivizes network participants to contribute computational power to secure the network. This mining process involves solving complex mathematical problems using specialized hardware, and is what allows the Bitcoin network to verify transactions and maintain its security.

Conclusion

Satoshi Nakamoto's technical skills were essential in the development of the Bitcoin protocol. The hashing algorithm, proof of work system, scripting language, P2P network, and mining process were all critical components in creating a decentralized system that was resistant to censorship and control by any central authority. Satoshi's technical expertise allowed for the creation of a new digital currency that has the potential to revolutionize the way we think about money and transactions.

Chapter 5: The Creation of Bitcoin
Early Stages of Development

Satoshi Nakamoto's creation of Bitcoin was a long and complex process that involved several stages of development. In this chapter, we will examine the early stages of Bitcoin's development, from the initial concept to the creation of the first Bitcoin software.

The Idea

The idea for Bitcoin began with a paper published by Satoshi Nakamoto in 2008. The paper, titled "Bitcoin: A Peer-to-Peer Electronic Cash System," outlined a system for creating a decentralized digital currency that could be transferred between users without the need for a central authority.

The paper proposed the use of a digital ledger called the blockchain, which would record all Bitcoin transactions and ensure their validity through a process called mining. Miners would compete to solve complex mathematical problems, and the first miner to solve the problem would receive a reward in Bitcoin.

The idea of a decentralized currency had been explored before, but Satoshi's paper was unique in its proposed use of a blockchain and the consensus mechanism of mining. This combination made Bitcoin the first practical implementation of a decentralized digital currency.

The Development Team

After publishing the Bitcoin paper, Satoshi began working on the development of the Bitcoin software. Although Satoshi is credited with the creation of Bitcoin, it was not a one-person project. Several other developers, including Hal Finney and Martti Malmi, played important roles in the early stages of Bitcoin's development.

Hal Finney was the first person to receive a Bitcoin transaction from Satoshi, and he was instrumental in testing and improving the Bitcoin software. Finney was an experienced cryptographer and computer programmer, and he made several significant contributions to the development of Bitcoin.

Martti Malmi, a Finnish computer science student, was also an early contributor to the development of Bitcoin. Malmi worked closely with Satoshi to develop the initial Bitcoin software and was responsible for implementing several key features.

The First Bitcoin Software

In January 2009, Satoshi released the first version of the Bitcoin software, which was available for download on the internet. The software allowed users to mine Bitcoin and make transactions using the digital currency.

The first version of the Bitcoin software was simple compared to later versions, and it lacked many of the features that are now standard in Bitcoin wallets. However, it was a significant milestone in the development of Bitcoin and laid the foundation for future improvements.

The early Bitcoin software was tested by a small group of enthusiasts who were interested in the idea of a decentralized digital currency. These early users provided feedback on the software and helped to identify bugs and other issues.

The Genesis Block

On January 3, 2009, Satoshi created the first Bitcoin block, known as the Genesis Block. The block contained a message referencing a newspaper headline from that day, which read "Chancellor on brink of second bailout for banks." This message was interpreted by many as a commentary on the failures of the traditional banking system and a statement of the potential for Bitcoin to provide a better alternative.

The creation of the Genesis Block was an important milestone in the development of Bitcoin, as it represented the first use of the blockchain. The block contained the first

Bitcoin transaction, in which Satoshi sent 50 Bitcoin to Hal Finney.

Conclusion

The early stages of Bitcoin's development were marked by innovation and collaboration. Satoshi Nakamoto's paper proposed a radical new concept for a decentralized digital currency, and a group of dedicated developers worked together to turn that concept into a reality. The release of the first Bitcoin software and the creation of the Genesis Block marked important milestones in the development of Bitcoin and set the stage for future growth and innovation.

The Genesis Block

The creation of Bitcoin began with the release of its first software version, which contained the genesis block. This genesis block serves as the starting point for the entire blockchain, and it is the first block in the Bitcoin network.

The genesis block was created by Satoshi Nakamoto on January 3, 2009. This block is unique in that it contains a special message that has been interpreted as a political statement. The message reads, "The Times 03/Jan/2009 Chancellor on brink of second bailout for banks." This statement refers to a headline from The Times newspaper, which was published on the same day that the genesis block was created.

The inclusion of this message in the genesis block has been seen as a symbolic gesture, and it has been interpreted in different ways. Some see it as a criticism of the traditional banking system and a call for a decentralized alternative. Others see it as a historical marker, signifying the birth of Bitcoin and its potential impact on the financial world.

The genesis block is unique in that it has no previous block to reference, as it is the first block in the chain. This means that it does not contain a hash pointer to a previous block, which is a crucial component of the blockchain. Instead, the genesis block's hash is hardcoded into the

Bitcoin software, making it an exception to the normal rules of block validation.

The creation of the genesis block was a significant milestone in the development of Bitcoin. It marked the beginning of a new era in decentralized technology and has paved the way for the growth and evolution of the cryptocurrency industry.

The genesis block's creation also demonstrated Satoshi Nakamoto's technical expertise in cryptography and computer science. The ability to create a secure and decentralized system such as Bitcoin required an understanding of advanced concepts in these fields.

In addition to its technical significance, the genesis block has also become a cultural icon within the Bitcoin community. The message contained in the block has been widely referenced and analyzed, and the block itself has been used in artwork, merchandise, and other forms of creative expression.

Overall, the creation of the genesis block is a critical moment in the history of Bitcoin and represents the beginning of a new era in decentralized technology. It serves as a symbol of Satoshi Nakamoto's vision and technical expertise, and it continues to inspire and shape the development of the cryptocurrency industry today.

First Transactions

Bitcoin's first transactions were pivotal in shaping the currency's trajectory and cementing its position as a legitimate form of digital currency. In this section, we'll delve into the details of the first transactions ever made with Bitcoin and the impact they had on the currency's growth.

The first Bitcoin transaction was made on January 12, 2009, when Satoshi Nakamoto sent 10 Bitcoins to Hal Finney, a renowned cryptographer and computer programmer. This transaction is widely considered to be the first-ever transaction made with Bitcoin and is often referred to as the "genesis transaction."

It's worth noting that the first Bitcoin block had already been mined on January 3, 2009, but it wasn't until Nakamoto's transaction with Finney that Bitcoin had any value or use beyond its technical novelty.

The second-ever Bitcoin transaction was also made by Nakamoto, who sent 10 Bitcoins to a developer named Martti Malmi on January 12, 2009. Malmi was one of the earliest adopters of Bitcoin, and his contribution to the currency's development was significant.

After these initial transactions, Bitcoin started to gain traction in online communities and forums dedicated to cryptography and digital currencies. People began to mine

Bitcoins and trade them on online exchanges, and by the end of 2009, the value of a single Bitcoin had risen from essentially zero to $0.008.

The first known commercial transaction involving Bitcoin took place on May 22, 2010, when a programmer named Laszlo Hanyecz purchased two Papa John's pizzas for 10,000 Bitcoins. This transaction is widely considered to be the first instance of Bitcoin being used to purchase a physical good or service, and it set the stage for Bitcoin's use in commercial transactions.

As more and more people began to use Bitcoin, the currency's value continued to rise. In 2011, it reached parity with the US dollar, and by 2013, its value had surged to over $1,000 per Bitcoin. This exponential growth in value attracted even more users and investors to the currency, and it sparked a wave of innovation in the blockchain and cryptocurrency industries.

However, Bitcoin's early days were not without controversy. In 2011, an online marketplace called Silk Road emerged, which allowed users to buy and sell illegal drugs and other illicit goods using Bitcoin. The use of Bitcoin on Silk Road highlighted the currency's potential for illegal activities and raised concerns about its regulation.

Despite these challenges, Bitcoin continued to gain acceptance and use in both legal and illegal activities. Today, Bitcoin is a widely recognized and accepted form of digital currency, and it has paved the way for the development of numerous other cryptocurrencies and blockchain-based technologies.

In conclusion, the first transactions made with Bitcoin were instrumental in establishing the currency's value and potential. From Nakamoto's initial transactions with Finney and Malmi to Hanyecz's purchase of pizza with 10,000 Bitcoins, these early transactions set the stage for Bitcoin's use in commercial transactions and sparked a wave of innovation and development in the blockchain and cryptocurrency industries.

Chapter 6: The Launch of Bitcoin
The Bitcoin Whitepaper

The Bitcoin whitepaper, titled "Bitcoin: A Peer-to-Peer Electronic Cash System," was published in October 2008 by a person or group of people using the pseudonym Satoshi Nakamoto. The whitepaper outlined the technical details of a decentralized digital currency system that would allow individuals to send and receive electronic payments without the need for intermediaries like banks or payment processors.

The whitepaper opened with a brief history of electronic payments, highlighting the limitations of existing systems like credit cards and PayPal. It then introduced the concept of a decentralized peer-to-peer network that would allow users to exchange value without the need for trust in any central authority.

The key innovation of the Bitcoin whitepaper was the introduction of the blockchain, a distributed ledger that records all Bitcoin transactions in chronological order. The blockchain is maintained by a network of nodes that validate transactions and update the ledger in a decentralized manner.

The whitepaper also introduced the concept of mining, a process by which nodes compete to solve complex mathematical problems in order to validate transactions and add new blocks to the blockchain. Miners are rewarded with newly created bitcoins for their efforts, and this incentivizes them to participate in the network and ensure its security.

The whitepaper described how the system would prevent double-spending, a problem that had plagued previous attempts at creating digital currencies. By using cryptographic proof and timestamping, the blockchain ensures that each Bitcoin can only be spent once.

The whitepaper also outlined the supply and distribution of bitcoins. The total supply of bitcoins is limited to 21 million, and new bitcoins are created at a decreasing rate over time. The whitepaper proposed that early adopters would be rewarded with higher amounts of bitcoins, but noted that this would be balanced out by the long-term benefits of wider adoption and increased transaction volume.

The Bitcoin whitepaper was well-received by the cryptography and computer science communities, and it sparked a flurry of activity among developers and enthusiasts who saw the potential of a decentralized digital currency system. In January 2009, the first Bitcoin software was released, and the network went live shortly thereafter.

The publication of the Bitcoin whitepaper marked the beginning of a new era in the world of finance and technology. It paved the way for the creation of hundreds of new cryptocurrencies and decentralized applications, and it has inspired countless people to explore the possibilities of blockchain technology. Despite its many challenges and controversies, Bitcoin remains the most widely recognized and influential cryptocurrency in the world, and the legacy of its whitepaper continues to shape the evolution of the digital economy.

Initial Reception and Adoption

The launch of Bitcoin in 2009 marked the beginning of a new era of decentralized digital currency. Satoshi's creation was met with a mixture of curiosity, skepticism, and excitement, and its early adoption was slow but steady. In this section, we will explore the initial reception of Bitcoin and its early adopters.

Early Reception

The release of the Bitcoin whitepaper in 2008 was met with relatively little attention at first. It was only after the first block was mined and the network went live in January 2009 that the potential of this new technology began to attract attention from the broader public. The first Bitcoin exchange, called "New Liberty Standard," was launched in October 2009, setting the exchange rate at 1,309 BTC to $1 USD.

Early adopters were largely tech enthusiasts and libertarians who were attracted to the idea of a decentralized, censorship-resistant currency. Many saw Bitcoin as a potential replacement for traditional financial institutions and a way to bypass government regulation and control.

Adoption by Merchants

In the early days of Bitcoin, the primary use case was for peer-to-peer transactions between individuals. However, as more people became interested in the currency, merchants began to take notice. In May 2010, the first documented purchase using Bitcoin was made when a programmer named Laszlo Hanyecz bought two pizzas for 10,000 BTC (worth approximately $600 million at today's prices). This event is now celebrated as "Bitcoin Pizza Day" in the cryptocurrency community.

In the following months, more merchants began to accept Bitcoin as a form of payment. One of the early adopters was the online marketplace, Silk Road, which allowed users to buy and sell illegal goods anonymously using Bitcoin. While the use of Bitcoin on Silk Road was controversial, it helped to demonstrate the potential of the currency as a means of conducting anonymous transactions.

Mainstream Attention

As Bitcoin continued to gain adoption, it also began to attract attention from mainstream media and financial institutions. In 2011, the popular technology blog, Slashdot, featured a post on Bitcoin, which helped to raise awareness of the currency among tech enthusiasts. The same year, Forbes published an article titled "Crypto-Currency: Bitcoin," which provided a detailed explanation of how Bitcoin worked and its potential applications.

In 2013, the value of Bitcoin skyrocketed, reaching an all-time high of over $1,000 USD. This sudden increase in value led to a surge in media attention, with outlets such as CNN, The Wall Street Journal, and The New York Times all reporting on the currency. The increased attention also attracted investment from venture capitalists, who saw the potential for Bitcoin to disrupt the financial industry.

Conclusion

The early adoption of Bitcoin was slow but steady, driven by a community of tech enthusiasts and libertarians who saw the potential of a decentralized, censorship-resistant currency. Over time, the currency began to attract attention from mainstream media and financial institutions, leading to increased adoption and investment. Today, Bitcoin and other cryptocurrencies have become an important part of the financial landscape, with a market capitalization of over $2 trillion USD.

The Bitcoin Community

The creation of Bitcoin not only introduced a revolutionary new technology but also brought together a community of individuals who shared a common interest in the potential of this digital currency. Satoshi Nakamoto, as the creator of Bitcoin, was the central figure in this community in the early days, but as interest in Bitcoin grew, so did the community.

In the early days of Bitcoin, the community was relatively small and consisted primarily of developers, cryptography enthusiasts, and libertarians. The community was very active on forums such as Bitcointalk and the Bitcoin mailing list, where they discussed the technical aspects of Bitcoin and its potential applications. The community was also responsible for the development of the first Bitcoin software clients and the establishment of the first Bitcoin exchanges.

One of the key characteristics of the Bitcoin community is its decentralized nature. There is no single entity or organization that controls Bitcoin, and the community operates through a consensus-based model. Decisions related to the development and direction of Bitcoin are made through open discussion and community consensus, with no central authority or decision-making body.

As Bitcoin grew in popularity and adoption, the community became more diverse and inclusive. More individuals from different backgrounds and professions became interested in Bitcoin and its potential applications. This led to the emergence of new sub-communities within the larger Bitcoin community, such as merchants, investors, and academics.

Another important aspect of the Bitcoin community is its strong emphasis on privacy and security. As a decentralized currency, Bitcoin is designed to be resistant to censorship and government control, and the community is dedicated to maintaining this feature. The community has also been at the forefront of developing new technologies such as the Tor network and VPNs to enhance privacy and security in the use of Bitcoin.

Despite the decentralized nature of the Bitcoin community, there have been instances of controversy and disagreement. One of the most notable was the block size debate, which centered around the issue of how to scale Bitcoin to accommodate the growing number of users and transactions. This debate led to the formation of different factions within the community and ultimately resulted in the creation of Bitcoin Cash, a hard fork of Bitcoin.

Overall, the Bitcoin community has played a crucial role in the growth and development of Bitcoin. Its decentralized and consensus-based approach to decision-making, its emphasis on privacy and security, and its inclusiveness and diversity have all contributed to making Bitcoin a truly revolutionary technology.

Chapter 7: The Mystery of Satoshi Nakamoto
Satoshi's Identity

Satoshi Nakamoto is the pseudonym used by the creator(s) of Bitcoin, and their true identity remains a mystery to this day. Despite numerous attempts by journalists, researchers, and internet sleuths, the person or group behind Satoshi Nakamoto has never been definitively identified.

The mystery surrounding Satoshi's identity has only added to the allure of Bitcoin and its creator. Some have speculated that Satoshi is a group of people rather than an individual, while others have suggested that Satoshi could be a government agency or a well-funded corporation.

There have been several individuals who have claimed to be Satoshi Nakamoto over the years, but none of these claims have been verified. One of the most prominent of these claimants is Craig Wright, an Australian computer scientist and businessman who has been involved in the cryptocurrency space for several years.

Wright first claimed to be Satoshi Nakamoto in 2016, but his claim was met with widespread skepticism from the Bitcoin community. He later provided what he claimed was cryptographic proof of his identity, but this proof was also widely criticized as being fraudulent.

Despite the lack of concrete evidence, the search for Satoshi Nakamoto has continued, with some even offering large sums of money as a reward for information that leads to their identification. However, many in the Bitcoin community believe that Satoshi's identity should remain a mystery, as it adds to the decentralized nature of the currency and ensures that no one individual or group can hold too much power over the system.

Possible Candidates for Satoshi Nakamoto

Over the years, there have been several individuals who have been identified as potential candidates for the identity of Satoshi Nakamoto. These individuals have been identified based on their technical expertise, involvement in the early development of Bitcoin, and other circumstantial evidence.

One of the earliest identified candidates was Dorian Nakamoto, a Japanese-American man who lived in California. In 2014, a Newsweek article claimed that Dorian was the creator of Bitcoin, but he denied the claim and stated that he had never heard of the currency before the article was published.

Another potential candidate is Hal Finney, a computer programmer who was involved in the development of PGP encryption and was one of the first people to download and run the Bitcoin software. Finney passed away in 2014, but before his death, he denied that he was Satoshi Nakamoto.

Nick Szabo, a computer scientist and cryptographer, is also considered a possible candidate for the identity of Satoshi Nakamoto. Szabo is known for his work on digital contracts and has been referred to as the "father of smart contracts." He has never publicly claimed to be Satoshi Nakamoto, but some have pointed to similarities between his writing and that of Satoshi Nakamoto.

Finally, there is the possibility that Satoshi Nakamoto is not an individual at all, but rather a group of people working together anonymously. This theory is supported by the fact that the whitepaper and early code for Bitcoin were written in excellent English, which some have suggested may have required input from multiple individuals.

Conclusion

The mystery surrounding Satoshi Nakamoto's identity has persisted for over a decade, and it is unlikely that it will ever be definitively solved. While some have claimed to be Satoshi Nakamoto, none of these claims have been verified, and the true identity of the creator(s) of Bitcoin remains a mystery.

However, the identity of Satoshi Nakamoto is ultimately less important than the impact that Bitcoin and other cryptocurrencies have had on the world. Satoshi's vision for a decentralized, peer-to-peer electronic cash system has changed the way we think about money and financial transactions, and has paved the way for new forms of digital assets and decentralized technologies.

The legacy of Satoshi Nakamoto will continue to be felt for years to come, regardless of their true identity. Their creation of Bitcoin and the subsequent growth of the cryptocurrency market has sparked a revolution in the world of finance and technology, disrupting traditional systems and empowering individuals to take control of their own assets and transactions. Satoshi's vision of a decentralized system free from government and corporate control has inspired countless others to explore new possibilities for blockchain and other decentralized technologies. In this way, the impact of Satoshi's work goes far beyond the creation of a single cryptocurrency and has opened up a new frontier in the world of technology and finance.

Rumors and Speculation

Since the launch of Bitcoin in 2009, there has been much speculation and rumor surrounding the identity of its creator, Satoshi Nakamoto. Despite numerous attempts to uncover their true identity, Satoshi remains anonymous to this day. However, this has not stopped rumors and speculation from circulating, with many people claiming to know who Satoshi really is.

One of the most persistent rumors surrounding Satoshi's identity is that they are a group of people rather than a single individual. The idea of a group of people working together to create Bitcoin is not unfounded, given the complexity of the project and the range of skills required. However, there is no concrete evidence to support this theory, and it remains purely speculative.

Another popular theory is that Satoshi Nakamoto is actually a pseudonym for a well-known individual or organization. Many names have been put forward over the years, including Nick Szabo, Hal Finney, and even the NSA. However, none of these claims have been substantiated, and the true identity of Satoshi remains a mystery.

Some have suggested that Satoshi Nakamoto is actually a government agency or a large corporation. This theory is based on the idea that Bitcoin's creation was too sophisticated and well-funded to have been the work of a single individual or small group of people. However, there is no evidence to support this theory, and it is generally dismissed by those who believe in the decentralized nature of Bitcoin and other cryptocurrencies.

Despite the lack of concrete evidence, the speculation and rumors surrounding Satoshi's identity continue to be a topic of interest and discussion within the cryptocurrency community. Some argue that knowing the true identity of Satoshi could help to legitimize Bitcoin in the eyes of mainstream institutions and governments, while others argue that the anonymity of Satoshi is an important part of the decentralized nature of Bitcoin.

In recent years, several individuals have come forward claiming to be Satoshi Nakamoto. In 2014, Newsweek claimed to have uncovered the true identity of Satoshi, naming a man named Dorian Nakamoto as the creator of Bitcoin. However, this claim was later debunked, with Dorian Nakamoto denying any involvement in the creation of Bitcoin.

In 2016, Australian entrepreneur Craig Wright claimed to be Satoshi Nakamoto, providing what he claimed was proof of his identity. However, his claims were met with skepticism by the cryptocurrency community, and no conclusive evidence was ever presented.

The identity of Satoshi Nakamoto may never be known, but their legacy lives on through the creation of Bitcoin and the wider cryptocurrency ecosystem. While the focus on Satoshi's identity can be intriguing, it is ultimately less important than the impact that Bitcoin has had on the world. Satoshi's vision for a decentralized, peer-to-peer electronic cash system has changed the way we think about money and financial transactions, and has paved the way for new forms of digital assets and decentralized technologies.

The Search for the Truth

The search for the true identity of Satoshi Nakamoto has been ongoing since the creation of Bitcoin. Many have attempted to unmask the mysterious figure, and numerous individuals have been accused of being Satoshi. However, to this day, the true identity of Satoshi remains a mystery.

One of the earliest clues to Satoshi's identity was the name used to register the bitcoin.org domain in August 2008. The domain registration listed "Satoshi Nakamoto" as the owner, but it is widely believed that this was a pseudonym. Some have speculated that the name is a combination of two prominent Japanese companies, "Satoshi" from SONY and "Nakamoto" from Nakamichi.

Another early clue was the language used in Satoshi's initial white paper, which demonstrated a mastery of English but contained certain phrases and idioms that suggested a non-native speaker. Some have suggested that Satoshi may be of European or Asian descent, and others have pointed to the use of British English spellings in certain communications as evidence that Satoshi may be British.

Over the years, a number of individuals have been suspected of being Satoshi Nakamoto, with varying degrees of evidence to support these claims. In 2014, Newsweek published an article claiming that a man named Dorian

Satoshi Nakamoto was the creator of Bitcoin. The article cited circumstantial evidence, such as the fact that Dorian had changed his name from Satoshi and had a background in engineering and computer programming. However, Dorian vehemently denied any involvement in Bitcoin and has since filed a lawsuit against Newsweek.

Other individuals who have been accused of being Satoshi include Hal Finney, a cryptographer who was an early supporter of Bitcoin, and Nick Szabo, a computer scientist who has been credited with developing the concept of smart contracts. However, both Finney and Szabo have denied being Satoshi and have pointed to various flaws in the evidence used to support these claims.

In 2014, Australian entrepreneur Craig Wright claimed that he was Satoshi Nakamoto, but his claims were met with widespread skepticism and criticism. Despite providing what he claimed was cryptographic proof of his identity, Wright was unable to convince the Bitcoin community that he was indeed the creator of the cryptocurrency.

Some have suggested that the true identity of Satoshi Nakamoto may never be revealed. It is possible that Satoshi was a group of individuals rather than a single person, or that the creator of Bitcoin took extreme measures to conceal their identity. Whatever the case may be, the mystery of Satoshi Nakamoto has only added to the intrigue and fascination surrounding the creation of Bitcoin.

Conclusion

Satoshi's Impact on the World

Satoshi Nakamoto's impact on the world has been significant and far-reaching, despite the fact that his identity remains unknown. His creation of Bitcoin and the underlying blockchain technology have revolutionized the way we think about money and financial transactions, and have paved the way for new forms of digital assets and decentralized technologies.

One of the most significant impacts of Satoshi's work has been the creation of a new decentralized financial system. Before the advent of Bitcoin, financial transactions were largely controlled by centralized institutions such as banks and governments. This meant that individuals had limited control over their money and financial transactions, and were often subject to high fees and slow processing times. With the creation of Bitcoin and other cryptocurrencies, however, individuals can now conduct financial transactions directly with one another, without the need for intermediaries. This has created a more democratic and transparent financial system that is accessible to anyone with an internet connection.

Another significant impact of Satoshi's work has been the rise of blockchain technology. While initially developed to power Bitcoin, blockchain technology has since been applied to a wide range of industries and use cases. This technology enables secure, transparent, and tamper-proof data storage and transactions, and has the potential to disrupt a wide range of industries, from supply chain management to voting systems.

Satoshi's work has also sparked a new wave of innovation in the tech industry. The creation of Bitcoin and blockchain technology has inspired countless entrepreneurs and developers to explore new ways to use decentralized technologies to solve real-world problems. This has led to the development of new digital assets, decentralized finance applications, and even new types of governance systems.

In addition to these technical innovations, Satoshi's work has also had a significant impact on the social and political landscape. By creating a decentralized financial system that is not subject to government or corporate control, Satoshi has given individuals more control over their financial lives. This has the potential to disrupt the current power structures that govern the global economy, and to empower individuals to take control of their financial destinies.

Satoshi's impact on the world can also be seen in the way that his work has sparked new conversations about the nature of money and value. With the rise of Bitcoin and other cryptocurrencies, people are questioning the traditional concepts of money and currency, and exploring new ideas about what constitutes value. This has led to new discussions about the role of money in our lives, and how we can use technology to create a more equitable and sustainable financial system.

Despite the many challenges that still exist in the world of cryptocurrencies and blockchain technology, there is no doubt that Satoshi's work has had a profound impact on the world. His vision for a decentralized financial system has inspired a new wave of innovation and entrepreneurship, and has given individuals more control over their financial lives. As we look to the future, it is clear that the legacy of Satoshi Nakamoto will continue to shape the world for years to come.

Continuing Influence of Bitcoin

Bitcoin has already had a significant impact on the world, but its influence is likely to continue for many years to come. In this section, we will explore some of the ways in which Bitcoin and its underlying technology could continue to shape the world in the future.

Firstly, Bitcoin has the potential to revolutionize the global financial system. As we discussed earlier, Bitcoin allows for fast, secure, and low-cost transactions without the need for intermediaries like banks or payment processors. This has the potential to disrupt traditional financial institutions and create a more open, transparent, and inclusive financial system.

Secondly, Bitcoin and other cryptocurrencies could continue to be used as a store of value and a hedge against inflation. In countries where the national currency is subject to inflation or instability, Bitcoin has already emerged as a popular alternative. This trend is likely to continue, as more people seek out alternative forms of money that are not subject to the whims of central banks or governments.

Thirdly, the underlying blockchain technology that powers Bitcoin could have numerous other applications beyond just financial transactions. For example, blockchains could be used to create secure, decentralized systems for voting, identity verification, or supply chain management. These applications have the potential to improve efficiency, transparency, and security in a wide range of industries.

Finally, the continued development and adoption of Bitcoin and other cryptocurrencies could have a significant impact on global power dynamics. As we have seen, Bitcoin's decentralized nature means that it is not subject to the control of any one government or institution. This has the potential to disrupt the traditional power structures that have governed the global economy for centuries.

In conclusion, while Bitcoin's impact on the world is already significant, its continuing influence could be even more profound. From revolutionizing the financial system to disrupting traditional power structures, Bitcoin and its underlying technology have the potential to shape the world in ways that we are only just beginning to imagine. As we move into an increasingly digital and decentralized future, it is likely that Bitcoin and other cryptocurrencies will play an increasingly important role in our lives.

What's Next for the Crypto Revolution

As the world continues to shift towards a digital-first economy, cryptocurrencies and blockchain technologies are becoming increasingly relevant. While Bitcoin was the first major application of these technologies, it certainly won't be the last.

One of the biggest trends in the cryptocurrency space is the rise of decentralized finance (DeFi). DeFi applications are built on top of blockchain technologies, and allow for peer-to-peer lending, borrowing, and trading without the need for traditional financial intermediaries. These applications have the potential to drastically reduce costs and increase financial inclusion for individuals around the world.

Another area of innovation in the cryptocurrency space is non-fungible tokens (NFTs). NFTs are unique digital assets that are built on top of blockchain technologies, and are being used for everything from digital art to sports collectibles. NFTs have the potential to revolutionize the way we think about ownership and value in the digital world.

Finally, governments around the world are starting to explore the potential of central bank digital currencies (CBDCs). CBDCs would be digital versions of traditional fiat currencies, and could be used to increase financial inclusion, reduce costs, and make transactions faster and more efficient. However, they could also raise concerns around privacy and government surveillance.

Overall, the future of the crypto revolution is still uncertain, but one thing is clear: these technologies are here to stay. As individuals and institutions continue to explore their potential, we can expect to see new and innovative use cases emerge, and the impact of these technologies on the world to continue to grow.

THE END

Key Terms and Definitions

To help you better understand the language and concepts related to aging and older adults, below you will find a list of key terms and their definitions.

1. Satoshi Nakamoto: The pseudonym used by the anonymous creator(s) of Bitcoin.

2. Bitcoin: The first decentralized cryptocurrency, created by Satoshi Nakamoto in 2008.

3. Cryptography: The practice of secure communication in the presence of third parties.

4. Blockchain: A decentralized, digital ledger that records transactions in a tamper-resistant and secure manner.

5. Mining: The process of adding new transactions to the blockchain by solving complex mathematical equations in exchange for newly created bitcoins.

6. Decentralization: The process of distributing power and decision-making authority away from a central authority or control.

7. Peer-to-peer: A type of network where all nodes have equal power and communicate directly with each other, without the need for a central server or authority.

8. Cypherpunk: A movement advocating for the use of strong cryptography to protect privacy and individual freedom.

9. Digital signature: A mathematical technique used to verify the authenticity and integrity of digital messages or documents.

10. Hash function: A mathematical function that converts data of any size into a fixed-size output, which is unique and irreversible.

Supporting Materials

Introduction:

- Nakamoto, S. (2008). Bitcoin: A peer-to-peer electronic cash system. https://bitcoin.org/bitcoin.pdf

- Tapscott, D., & Tapscott, A. (2016). Blockchain revolution: How the technology behind bitcoin is changing money, business, and the world. Penguin.

Chapter 1: Childhood and Education:

- Popper, N. (2014). Digital gold: Bitcoin and the inside story of the misfits and millionaires trying to reinvent money. HarperCollins.

- Warr, P. G. (2019). The history of Bitcoin. Routledge.

Chapter 2: Satoshi's Early Career:

- Popper, N. (2014). Digital gold: Bitcoin and the inside story of the misfits and millionaires trying to reinvent money. HarperCollins.

- Vigna, P., & Casey, M. J. (2015). The age of cryptocurrency: How Bitcoin and digital money are challenging the global economic order. St. Martin's Press.

Chapter 3: Satoshi's Influences and Philosophy:

- Hughes, E. (1993). A Cypherpunk's Manifesto. https://www.activism.net/cypherpunk/manifesto.html

- Nakamoto, S. (2008). Bitcoin: A peer-to-peer electronic cash system. https://bitcoin.org/bitcoin.pdf

Chapter 4: Satoshi's Technical Skills:

- Antonopoulos, A. M. (2014). Mastering Bitcoin: Unlocking digital cryptocurrencies. O'Reilly Media, Inc.

- Narayanan, A., Bonneau, J., Felten, E., Miller, A., & Goldfeder, S. (2016). Bitcoin and Cryptocurrency Technologies: A Comprehensive Introduction. Princeton University Press.

Chapter 5: The Creation of Bitcoin:

- Popper, N. (2014). Digital gold: Bitcoin and the inside story of the misfits and millionaires trying to reinvent money. HarperCollins.

- Nakamoto, S. (2008). Bitcoin: A peer-to-peer electronic cash system. https://bitcoin.org/bitcoin.pdf

Chapter 6: The Launch of Bitcoin:

- Popper, N. (2014). Digital gold: Bitcoin and the inside story of the misfits and millionaires trying to reinvent money. HarperCollins.

- Vigna, P., & Casey, M. J. (2015). The age of cryptocurrency: How Bitcoin and digital money are challenging the global economic order. St. Martin's Press.

Chapter 7: The Mystery of Satoshi Nakamoto:

- Popper, N. (2014). Digital gold: Bitcoin and the inside story of the misfits and millionaires trying to reinvent money. HarperCollins.

- Goodman, L. (2011). Growing up Bitcoin. Gawker. https://gawker.com/5847197/growing-up-bitcoin

Conclusion:

- Tapscott, D., & Tapscott, A. (2016). Blockchain revolution: How the technology behind bitcoin is changing money, business, and the world. Penguin.
- Casey, M. J., & Vigna, P. (2018). The truth machine: The blockchain and the future of everything. St. Martin's Press..